MIGRANTS
& MIGRATION

Peter Holden and Mike Langman
Introduction by Bill Oddie

HAMLYN

To Andrew and James

First published in 1994 by Hamlyn Limited,
an imprint of Reed Consumer Books Limited
Michelin House, 81 Fulham Road, London SW3 6RB
and Auckland, Melbourne, Singapore and Toronto.

Copyright © Reed International Books Limited 1994

Text copyright © Peter Holden 1994
Illustrations copyright © Mike Langman 1994
Photographs copyright © *see page 48.*

ISBN 0 600 57964 6

A CIP catalogue record for this book is available from
the British Library.

Cover photograph: Arctic Tern by M Hunt (RSPB)
Back cover photograph: C H Gomersall (RSPB)
Cover illustrations by Mike Langman
Printed in Hong Kong

CONTENTS

BILL ODDIE'S INTRODUCTION   4

INTRODUCTION   5

WHAT IS BIRD MIGRATION?   6

AMAZING FLIGHTS   10

WHY MIGRATE?   12

DISCOVERING MIGRATION   14

SOME SUMMER MIGRANTS   16

SOME WINTER MIGRANTS   18

THE EVOLUTION OF MIGRATION   20

MAKING THE JOURNEY   22

FINDING THEIR WAY   26

MIGRANTS OFF COURSE   30

DANGEROUS JOURNEY   32

STUDYING MIGRATION   36

YOUR OWN MIGRATION PROJECTS   40

OTHER MIGRANTS   44

GLOSSARY   46

INDEX   47

PHOTOGRAPHIC CREDITS   48

BILL ODDIE'S INTRODUCTION

Grown ups love droning on about how different – and difficult – things were when they were young. Well, when it comes to birdwatching, it's true! I was about seven when I managed to persuade my Dad to buy me my first pair of binoculars. That was over 40 years ago and there were no bird magazines or specialist optical dealers. I was lucky I didn't end up with a plastic toy pair! In fact, my first binoculars were very good and lasted for years, so Dad must have taken good advice from somewhere.

But how did I learn about how and where to go birdwatching? And how did I know what I was looking at? The only identification book available was the *Observer's Book of Birds*, which didn't even have all the British birds in it, let alone pictures of them in all their plumages. The first 'modern' fieldguide came out in 1954 when I was thirteen.

I like to think, though, that by the time I became a teenager, I wasn't a bad birdwatcher. So, how did I do it? Well, nearly every day, I used to walk to the local woods and around the golf course (watching out for flying balls as well as birds). Every weekend, I'd cycle to the local reservoir or persuade my Dad to give me a lift. And I'd campaign to take our family holidays in Norfolk or Devon so I could see some new birds. I spent an amazing amount of time but, looking back, I probably wasted a lot, too, making mistakes I could have avoided if only there'd been books like this one.

This book deals with Migrants and Migration. I must confess, this is my favourite birdy subject of all. For a start, the fact that birds do migrate means that anything can turn up anywhere and, when you go out birdwatching, you never really know what you are going to see. And how do they do it? We now know that birds can navigate by using the stars, the Earth's magnetic force and so on. When I was a lad, I used to just look up and wonder!

Yes, things have changed but, whatever your age, there are three undeniable facts. Firstly, there are birds everywhere, even in the middle of a city. Secondly, there is no substitute for getting out there and seeing for yourself. And, thirdly, birdwatching is a hobby for life. I'm still at it. Never give it up.

Bill Oddie

INTRODUCTION

This book introduces a secret world. A world of travel. Not travel by aircraft, which follow schedules, but travel that involves millions of creatures moving across the surface of the earth. And it is hardly noticed by most people as they go about their daily lives.

In our comfortable, man-made homes we can easily forget the natural world beyond our doors. We see pictures of wildlife in magazines and on television, but how often do we go and look for ourselves?

Our ancestors were controlled by the seasons. The arrival of ducks and geese in the autumn were a food supply for many people. The men who trapped ducks for market knew the daily routines of their prey as well as any modern ornithologist; and the arrival of Nightingales, Swallows and Corncrakes in spring were welcomed as a sign that winter's rough weather was almost past and the warmth of summer was approaching.

But, as the towns grew, farming became more mechanized and the wild places were tamed. Birds and wildlife had less and less impact on our daily lives and now we can forget them altogether ... but should we?

Birds have travelled from continent to continent for tens of thousands of years. Their story is almost beyond belief. Their behaviour can still surprise the best scientists and, even more important, these birds indicate how healthy our planet is. If birds are in trouble then the environment is probably in trouble, too.

So, let us enter this secret world and discover some of the wonders of bird migration!

Humans have been able to fly in aircraft for less than 100 years. Birds have been flying from continent to continent for millions of years.

Years ago, people used duck decoys to catch large numbers of birds for the town markets.

WHAT IS BIRD MIGRATION?

Birds are the world's greatest travellers. Almost half of Europe's 600 species regularly fly from one area to another and back again. This is called migration and it is still one of the marvels of the natural world.

Migration is the regular movement to and from a particular area. The most common migrations are linked to the seasons of the year. 'One Swallow does not a summer make' is an old saying that reminds us that the arrival of Swallows has been looked forward to each year for many generations.

Swallows return to the British Isles each spring, usually in April. We call them **summer migrants**. They will stay for our summer and rear one, two or sometimes three broods of young. Then, in autumn, they will leave.

Swallows from the British Isles fly south through Europe, over the Mediterranean Sea into Africa and then south over the Sahara Desert, across the Equator to their winter quarters in South Africa; a journey of over 8000 km. In South Africa, our Swallows have a second summer. There will be

A Swallow's journey from South Africa to the British Isles takes about four weeks. It flies by day and gathers in large roosts at night.

Some Pochards breed in Britain, others migrate here for the winter from northern and eastern Europe.

Flocks of Redwings migrating at night call to each other as they fly to keep in contact in the dark.

African Swallows busy rearing young at that time, but ours will not breed until they have completed their return journey to the British Isles. Once back they will probably return to exactly the same nest site that they used the year before.

Not all birds migrate across the Equator. The Redwing breeds in northern Europe, Iceland and the Baltic Republics. In autumn, most of them migrate to southern or western Europe where the climate is milder and food is easier to find. Often they migrate at night and you may hear the thin calls of Redwing flocks on the first cold, still nights of October. For most people in the British Isles, therefore, the Redwing is a **winter migrant**: it arrives in autumn and departs in spring.

Summer and winter migrants can be quite obvious, but **partial migrants** are often overlooked. For species which breed over a wide area it is a good idea if some move and others stay. Often the more northerly birds will migrate while those farther south stay behind. Sometimes the young will leave and

the adults stay or one sex may leave and the other will stay behind.

Robins are partial migrants. In Britain, most stay with us for the whole year, but in continental Europe the northern robins are long haul migrants which spend winter around the Mediterranean. In Finland, Robins are summer visitors. In parts of Spain they are winter visitors. In Britain, continental Robins arrive on the east coast in autumn, but are seldom recognized as migrants.

Even the Robins in British gardens are not all residents. After breeding, males and females split up and defend their territories. Females tend to wander away from their summer territory and some from southern England may travel to France for the winter.

The winter weather in the centre of a continent is much more severe than near the coast, which is influenced by the sea. The winter weather in eastern Europe and the Baltic Republics is too cold for many species, especially ducks which depend on open water, and waders which need soft mud. As a result there is large scale migration from the

Adult Shelducks leave their young and gather in flocks to moult.

continental interior towards the coasts. Birds such as Pochards, which visit British lakes and reservoirs, even close to town centres, may have spent the summer thousands of kilometres away to the east of Moscow.

So far, we have only looked at those birds which spend most of their lives on or near land, but seabirds are among the world's greatest migrants. Arctic Terns breed around the Arctic Circle (near the top of the world) and migrate to the oceans around the Antarctic Circle (at the bottom of the world).

Grey Wagtails like fast-flowing water. Even when rivers are slow-flowing, they tend to feed near weirs and similar places where water flows fastest.

This is an amazing 25,000-km round trip, and means they get to see more daylight than any other creature.

Shearwaters are also great migrants. Manx Shearwaters breed in western Europe and winter off the coast of Brazil in South America. One bird, ringed in Wales, made this journey in 16 days (an average speed of 30 km/hr or 740 km in a day). The Great Shearwater, which breeds on the Tristan da Cunha islands in the south Atlantic, has a circular migration route which takes it along the American coast to its moulting grounds off the coast of Newfoundland, returning via European and African coasts.

Many birds find better feeding conditions by flying thousands of kilometres. Some get the same advantage by just moving downhill. Grey Wagtails breed near fast flowing, rocky rivers and streams in upland and mountainous areas. In winter, they migrate downhill to feed beside lowland streams and rivers where there is less snow and ice and more food. This is called **altitudinal migration**.

Another form of migration is referred to as **leap-frog migration**. For example, those Ringed Plovers which nest near the Arctic, migrate farther than those that nest in Britain and central Europe. The northern birds pass through the area where the other

Lapwings need soft ground to reach their food and so a period of snow or frost will make them fly south in search of better conditions.

plovers are wintering to spend the winter much farther south.

Some wildfowl migrate for a very different reason: like other birds they need to moult and grow new feathers at regular intervals, usually once a year. While most birds moult gradually, many ducks and geese lose all their flight feathers at the same time, so they can't fly. Before moulting, some species go on a special **moult migration** to an area which is safe from predators and where there is a plentiful supply of food.

Traditionally, British Shelducks have migrated to the Heligoland Bight, off the coast of north-west Germany. Recently, however, Shelducks are forming new moulting areas, especially in Bridgewater Bay in Somerset and some other estuaries.

Birds make many journeys which scientists do not consider to be migration, but it is often difficult to be sure what is and is not.

Lapwings migrate to low-lying areas after they finish nesting. But if frost or snow makes it difficult for them to feed, they will move out of the area, usually travelling south or west in search of better conditions. In Spain, the Lapwing is known as *Ave Fria* (the bird of the frost) because its arrival so far south is an indication of cold weather. Such journeys are known as **cold weather movements**.

Tits may leave a wood in order to search for food in gardens: this is a **local migration**. Some birds, such as Kittiwakes, may leave their breeding colonies and go in a variety of directions: this is **dispersal**. Waxwings leave their breeding sites and wander in their search for food: this is called **nomadism**. Crossbills leave an area if food runs out and move into a new area where they may or may not stay and breed: this is an **irruption**.

An Arctic Tern (right) flies over good feeding areas on its way south in autumn.

Manx Shearwaters (below) spend the hours of daylight feeding out at sea. They approach their cliff-top nest burrows only after dark.

AMAZING FLIGHTS

Ruby-throated Hummingbirds are tiny, but they migrate 3400 km from North to central America, some making a 800 km flight across the Gulf of Mexico.

Blackpoll Warblers migrate from Canada to South America in one flight. The shortest route takes them away from the land and out over the Atlantic Ocean.

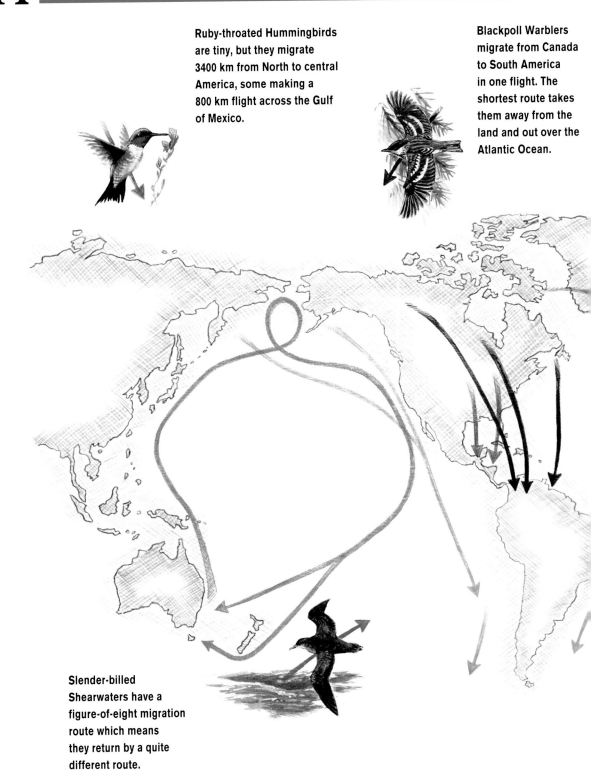

Slender-billed Shearwaters have a figure-of-eight migration route which means they return by a quite different route.

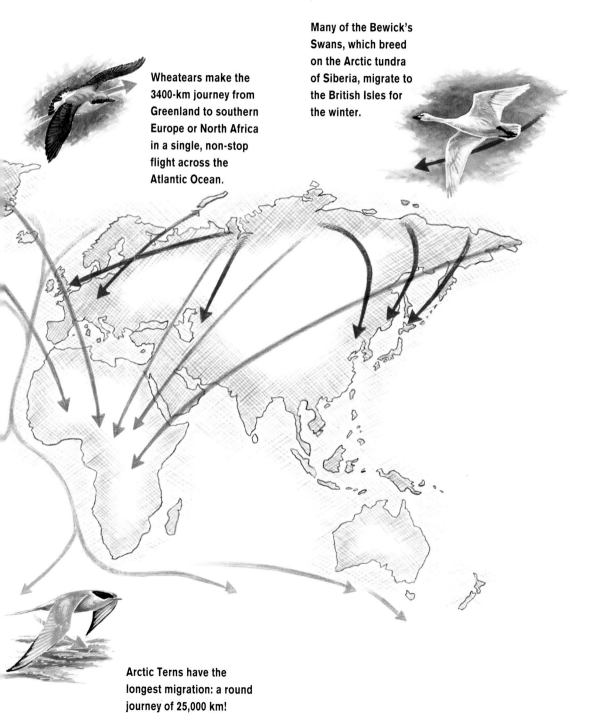

Many animals migrate, but flight gives birds greater freedom to move from one habitat to another or even from one continent to another. They have evolved different ways of storing fat to use as fuel and they use energy-saving methods to travel swiftly over land or sea. This map shows just a few of the spectacular migrations made by birds in different parts of the world.

Wheatears make the 3400-km journey from Greenland to southern Europe or North Africa in a single, non-stop flight across the Atlantic Ocean.

Many of the Bewick's Swans, which breed on the Arctic tundra of Siberia, migrate to the British Isles for the winter.

Arctic Terns have the longest migration: a round journey of 25,000 km!

WHY MIGRATE?

More Willow Warblers migrate to Europe than any other species.

Birds risk their lives when they migrate: they may run into bad weather or they may be attacked by predators, and there may be food shortages or drought at their journey's end. We know that many of the birds that set out on migration do not survive, so why do they do it? The answer is that the species benefits by migrating. Individual birds may not survive, but the whole species does better by undertaking this annual journey.

Every year, millions of Willow Warblers leave central and southern Africa and fly to the forests of northern Europe and Asia to breed. These forests are huge and they are full of the insect food which the warblers need to raise their young. But, while the forests are excellent summer homes, they are cold and dark in winter and the insects are hard to find. So, the warblers leave in the autumn and return to Africa.

Another advantage of moving away from the Equator to breed is that there is more

Some Dotterels (below) fly directly from Africa to their northerly breeding grounds. Others have regular stopping places, some of which have been in use for many years.

daylight. In summer in the Arctic there are almost 24 hours of daylight which means that birds, such as Bewick's Swans (which nest on the tundra of Siberia) have much more time to feed.

Bewick's Swans feed on the nutritious new plant growth of the Arctic and finish nesting and rear their young in a little over 100 days. The summer is short and they must leave before the snow and ice return.

The farther north birds live, the more difficult it becomes for them to survive all year round. Some, like Long-tailed Ducks stay and feed as long as there is ice-free water. Others, such as Snow Buntings, are specialists in finding seeds in areas blown free of snow.

In summer, there is food and lots of space for the birds migrating from the south so there is less competition for nesting sites and food. Because few birds live here all year round, new arrivals can stake a claim to the best territories.

Dotterels migrate from Africa to nest on the tops of the highest Scottish mountains. They wait on lowland fields for most of the snow and ice to melt and then return to the high tops to mark out and defend the best territories. Dotterels rarely face competition because other plovers (members of the same family) nest at lower levels.

Migration to the Arctic not only gives Barnacle Geese a supply of food, but also safe places to nest. Large ground-nesting birds, which are flightless when they moult, are in danger from ground predators such as foxes. But harsh Arctic winters restrict the number of predators and most nests escape unharmed.

Another reason for migrating is that certain places are ideal for nesting and, therefore, birds return to them year after year. Seabird colonies, for example, are full of birds for a short, hectic breeding season, but are largely deserted at other times. Suitable cliffs for Gannet colonies are not very common, but, once established, they may be used for hundreds, even thousands, of years.

Young Gannets swim and fly away from their colonies as soon as they are able to leave the cliffs. Most make their way to their wintering grounds off the west coast of Africa and may not return to the colony for a year or two. Many eventually return and, in time, will nest on the cliffs where they were hatched!

Many Ospreys live in tropical or semi-tropical areas. They feed on fish, which they catch by diving. In spring, some Ospreys leave the warm waters of the tropics and fly to more northerly feeding grounds where, for a time, there is plenty of food and little competition for it. But, away from the tropics the summer season is relatively short and in winter fish go deep, are hard to catch and inland lakes freeze, so Ospreys return to the tropics.

The feathers on the faces of Snow Buntings are often worn away by ice crystals. They have an extra moult and grow new face feathers before the breeding season starts.

In the Arctic, Barnacle Geese nest on rugged cliffs which gives them some extra protection from Arctic Foxes.

DISCOVERING MIGRATION

Most of the discoveries of migration have been made during the twentieth century, but the arrival and departure of migrants has been observed for thousands of years. Early observers did not always understand what they saw, but they marvelled at the seasonal changes and sometimes tried to explain them. First explanations for the arrival and departure of migrants were often wide of the mark, but sometimes they were accurate.

Drawings of migrant birds, notably Red-breasted and White-fronted Geese, appear on the walls of Egyptian tombs and probably date from around 3000 BC, but we do not know their significance. They may have been special birds because they appeared out of the North each year or they may have simply been good to eat!

The regular appearance of storks and Turtle Doves is referred to in the Old Testament of the Bible. Even today, the migration of thousands of White Storks around the eastern end of the Mediterranean is a marvellous wildlife spectacle. The arrival of Turtle Doves is less spectacular, but large numbers still pass through Israel. In Biblical times, they had special significance as a bird used for sacrifice.

Classical Greek writers of more than 2000 years ago were remarkably accurate in some of their observations. Aristotle wrote of Cranes which nested on the steppes north of the Black Sea and flew to the source of the Nile in central Africa. Aristotle also noted that Cuckoos left in July and that birds were fatter before migration. He was right!

But Aristotle was not always right. He also believed that Redstarts turned into Robins for the winter, and that Swallows and kites slept through the winter by hibernating in crevices. His writings were accepted as the truth for more than a thousand years!

Some early British writers reported the occasional arrival of large numbers of Crossbills. The irruption of Crossbills is now well-known to ornithologists and so the old reports are probably reliable. Other authors, however, wrote of Swallows submerging

Paintings in Egyptian tombs (left) are among the earliest known examples of bird illustrations.

'Angels', seen on radar during World War II, were a mystery until people realised they were migrating birds.

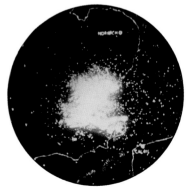

themselves in ponds for the winter! Other 'authorities' suggested that migrant birds flew to the Moon because they were not strong enough to undertake sea crossings! There were even popular stories of small birds riding on the backs of larger species and of Barnacles turning into geese for the winter. Even the first of the modern naturalists, Gilbert White, who lived in the eighteenth century, seemed to believe that Swallows hibernated in ponds, when he knew that other species migrated.

During the nineteenth and early twentieth centuries great strides were made in understanding migration. Various observers noted seasonal arrivals and departures. Migrant Swallows were seen over the sea, far from land, and, as world travel and specimen-collecting became more widespread, so the theory of migration became more accepted.

Ornithologists in both Britain and America were fascinated with the subject. In Britain, records were gathered from lighthouse keepers because large numbers of night-time migrants were attracted to these large, powerful lights. In addition, many collectors shot and stuffed migrating birds, especially rare migrants.

There were several early attempts to mark birds in some way. One of the first organized marking schemes was set-up in the late nineteenth century in Denmark. Similar schemes were established in Britain and other countries. Soon attaching a light-weight, numbered ring to the legs of individual birds became the basis of migration studies. Discoveries were made about where some birds spent the summer and winter, the routes they took and their life-span.

The use of radar during World War II showed that flocks of migrating birds could be seen. At first they were called 'angels' because they appeared where no plane should be. Soon ornithologists realized the value of these radar images as a method of tracing migration routes.

Over 2000 years ago, Aristotle wrote that Cranes flew to the source of the Nile in Africa for the winter. This was a remarkably accurate observation.

A Crossbill irruption was first recorded in Hertfordshire by Matthew Paris in 1251 (see page 9).

SOME SUMMER MIGRANTS

The summer sounds of our countryside are largely made up of the songs of summer migrants: the Cuckoo's call and the songs of Swallows and many warblers. After dark you may even hear Nightingales in southern England.

The first summer migrant to return from Africa is usually the Wheatear, which often arrives on our coasts in March. Chiffchaffs, which may have wintered around the Mediterranean, will arrive at about the same time. Willow Warblers and Swallows from

③

① Cuckoos arrive in April and adults leave in July, while young may stay until September. They lay their eggs in the nests of other species.

② Sedge Warblers arrive from Africa in April and leave in August and September. They nest in thick bushes near water.

③ Swifts arrive in late April or early May and leave in August. Most nest in roofs.

④ Garganeys are migratory ducks and are rare visitors to marshes in southern and eastern England. You may see them on migration in May.

Africa mainly return in April as will many other migrants. Swifts are often not back until early May and Spotted Flycatchers and Reed Warblers may be even later. By the end of May most migrants will be back and the summer breeding season will be under way.

Adult Cuckoos are often the first migrants to leave the British Isles after breeding: they generally go south in July. Swifts may leave in early August, and between then and the end of October all the other summer migrants will also depart.

⑤ **Swallows arrive in April and may stay until late October. They nest in sheds and barns, usually in the country.**

⑥ **Sand Martins arrive in March or April and leave in September. They nest in holes in banks or soft cliffs.**

⑦ **House Martins arrive in April and leave in October. They nest under the eaves of houses in towns and villages.**

⑧ **Blackcaps arrive in April and leave in September, but some are seen in winter. Experts think that these are migrants from elsewhere in Europe.**

SOME WINTER MIGRANTS

For birds that breed in the Arctic and in northern and eastern Europe, the winter weather in the British Isles seems mild. Most lakes are unfrozen, the soil is usually soft and there are plenty of feeding sites which are not covered in snow.

Some of the first migrants to arrive for the winter are partial migrants, and they may pass unnoticed. Lapwings from the continent arrive from late June and gather in small flocks. They will be joined by our own birds once they have finished nesting. During the

① A few Goldeneyes nest in Scotland but most come to Britain from northern Europe. They arrive in October and leave in March.

② Whooper Swans arrive from Iceland in October and return there in March.

③ Shovelers are here all year round, but those that nest here migrate south, while others from northern and eastern Europe arrive to take their place.

④ Short-eared Owls that nest in Britain often migrate to coastal marshes for the winter. Some from northern Europe migrate here.

summer other waders arrive from the north on our estuaries: Knots, Bar-tailed Godwits, Whimbrels and Grey Plovers feed in the rich mud. Some will stay for the winter, others will feed up and continue their journey.

Wild geese and swans arrive here in October, travelling in family groups. Small numbers of Redwings and Fieldfares (northern thrushes) nest here, but in October and November many more flock to the British Isles. First they feed on the plentiful supply of berries and, when the berries run out, they feed on worms and other small animals which live in the soil.

⑤ **Redwings arrive in October and leave in March. They nest in northern Europe and Iceland.**

⑥ **Fieldfares arrive in October and leave in March and April. A few do nest here, but most nest in northern and eastern Europe.**

⑦ **Bramblings arrive in October and leave around March, but the numbers that come here vary from year to year.**

⑧ **Great Spotted Woodpeckers are residents. In Britain, they seldom move more than a kilometre or two from where they hatch.**

THE EVOLUTION OF MIGRATION

Crested Tits, like this one above, are residents, mainly in the conifer woods of northern Europe.

FACTS

■ It is usual for a small migrant to fly non-stop for around 75 hours in order to cross the Mediterranean and the Sahara.

■ It has been estimated that well over five thousand million birds migrate to Africa each autumn!

■ Between four and five million birds are ringed each year.

Bramblings breed in northern forests, mostly in birch woods, but also on the edge of pine forests.

Migrating birds not only travel great distances, they cross oceans, deserts and mountains. Those that survive these incredible journeys find more food or good nesting conditions. But how did these migration journeys come about?

Bird migration has probably been taking place for millions of years. But, the migrations that take place in Europe today probably began about 11,000 years ago when the ice sheet which covered much of Europe, Asia and North America started to melt at the end of the last Ice Age.

The vegetation of Europe would have been very different then, even southern Europe would have had Arctic tundra. But, as the climate warmed and the ice retreated, the forests of birch and pine spread north and the birds such as Bramblings, which lived in them, also spread northwards. Crested Tits and other species which could find food all year round became residents but many, like the Willow Warbler which ate insects, spread into these new feeding areas to take advantage of the food and to rear young. When their food became scarce in autumn, and there was less daylight in which to feed, Willow Warblers and many other insect-eaters flew back to their original homes.

As the ice-cap retreated farther north, more land was revealed. The great land masses of the northern hemisphere, where there was no competition from other species, became available and birds like Wheatears were able to spread east into Asia and west into the north of North America (see the map on page 10).

Some of the species of birds that colonized the new areas were able to live there all year round and became residents. Some returned part of the way to places where the climate and food enabled them to survive the winter. But, for others, their home remained in Africa. So, after each breeding season they returned and their journeys became longer.

Rather than imagining that Swallows or Swifts are European birds which fly south for the winter, we should, perhaps, think of them as African birds which come north to take advantage of a temporary supply of food and then return home again! By staying in Africa they would be competing for food and nest sites with many similar species. By moving north, they find more food, better nest sites and more hours of daylight. As a result, they rear more young and, although they face dangers along the journey, enough birds survive to make it worthwhile and so they return the following year.

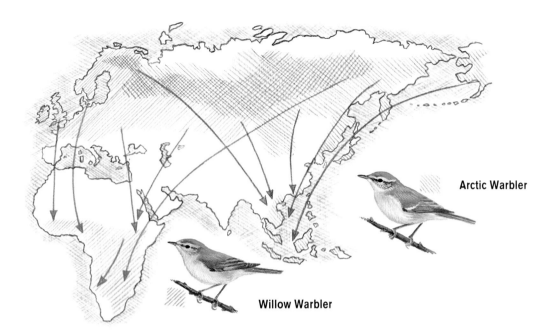

This map shows the breeding and wintering areas of Willow and Arctic Warblers: two closely related species which breed in similar areas, but have quite separate migrations. This is because one species was split by glaciation into two – an eastern and a western species.

Most of the migrants that visit Europe in spring travel from Africa where they spend the winter. There are similar patterns in Asia where birds, such as Arctic Warblers (which breed in the Baltic Republics in summer) spend winter in south-east Asia. Also, in North America, many summer migrants spend winter in Central or South America. Wheatears, which visit northern North America and originate in Europe or Africa, continue to return to their traditional homes.

During the long history of migration, some birds have changed their habits. The Barn Swallow of America is the same species as the Swallow of Europe and Africa. It, too, migrates, but it flies to South America. All Swallows once migrated to Africa, but presumably those in North America found that if they flew southwards (rather than follow traditional routes) they reached very similar habitats and travelled only half the distance. As there was less competition and more migrants survived, they would be able to return to their nesting areas earlier and fitter the following spring.

Ice covering Europe 11,000 years ago helped shape the landscape and changed bird migration patterns.

Making the Journey

Years before migration was understood, people knew that birds disappeared at one season and reappeared at another. But they could not imagine that these birds were capable of undertaking long journeys over land or sea, or of being able to fly at night. So, the fantastic theories developed that we have already read about. Even now it is one of the natural wonders of the world; how birds, both large and small, can find the energy to travel so far.

Before migration, Swallows become restless, there are changes in behaviour: they abandon territories and flock together. Together they set off in daylight and often fly into a headwind rather than have the wind behind them, presumably because it is easier to feed in these conditions.

Swallows feed as they fly and large groups of migrating Swallows gather at dusk to roost in a reedbed or some other safe place. While most of the distances between overnight roosts are quite short, there are times when direct, non-stop flight is needed: for the two sea crossings and the 1500-km flight across the Sahara Desert. For a Swallow, the journey from western Europe to southern Africa takes up to six weeks. The return in spring

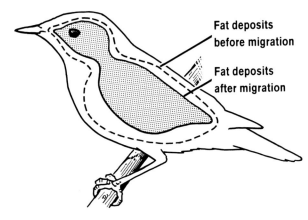

Fat deposits before migration

Fat deposits after migration

The area inside the dotted line (above) is where a Sedge Warbler stores its fat; the dark area shows how much weight it can lose during migration.

has more urgency with the breeding season approaching and may take four weeks.

Migrants that make long, non-stop flights need fuel. This fuel is fat which gives them the energy for prolonged flights. Before migration a bird defends a feeding territory and physical changes to its body allow fat storage cells around the body to enlarge and store quantities of extra fat. The amount of fat stored depends on the length of the journey to be flown.

Small migrants, which make long journeys, build up so much fat that they increase their

FACTS
- While most British Swallows leave in the autumn, very occasionally a few birds are seen in Britain in winter, especially in the south.
- Arctic Terns fly up to 17,500 km in each direction when migrating.

Swallows become more and more restless before migrating.

With so many large birds of prey together there is no opportunity for feeding on migration. These are Honey Buzzards with Black Kites.

weight by a half and some may double it. Ruby-throated Hummingbirds increase their body-weight by up to 50 per cent before they cross the Gulf of Mexico. Waders, about to fly from western Europe to their Arctic breeding grounds, put on similar amounts of weight. Sedge Warblers, which fly direct from from Britain to central Africa, may double their normal body weight before leaving.

Not all feeding takes place where the birds have spent the summer. Pied Flycatchers from northern Europe leave early and fly to Portugal or Spain. There, with more Pied Flycatchers and other migrants, they hold feeding territories for four to five weeks while they build up their fat reserves for the single flight over the Mediterranean and the Sahara, and on into Africa.

Large migratory birds are quite different. They soar to cross large distances. These large, day-flying migrants all have long, broad wings and include the bigger birds of prey such as buzzards and eagles, storks, cranes, pelicans and even cormorants. To soar, birds need thermals: upcurrents of warm air which create lift. Using thermals migrating birds hardly need to flap their wings, so they get to the greatest height with the minimum amount of energy.

Thermals form where the ground is heated more quickly than the surrounding area. This often happens on the side of a hill which is warmed by the sun. The warmer the weather, the more thermals, so there are more in the middle of the day.

Soaring birds often have well defined flightpaths because they follow the best routes. Following lines of hills, they pick up thermals and join other soaring migrants where the geography of the land brings them together: at the end of a range of hills or at the coast. In Pennsylvania, USA one hill known as Hawk Mountain is a famous watch point for migrating birds of prey. On average 17,000 raptors pass over it each year.

Soaring migrants avoid sea crossings because there are no thermals. They use the shortest sea crossing or a natural land bridge. There are a some very well-known places in the world which are used by vast

Soaring birds using thermals.

Pied Flycatchers disappear from woodland soon after nesting.

numbers of soaring migrants every spring and autumn.

The Mediterranean is a huge barrier to soaring birds when they leave Europe. The only natural route from western Europe is across the Strait of Gibraltar, which is used by 200,000 soaring migrants each year. For eastern European birds, their route takes them around the eastern Mediterranean, crossing the Bosporus near Istanbul in Turkey and continuing around the eastern end of the Mediterranean and into Africa via the head of the Red Sea.

In autumn at the Bosporus, the numbers of migrants can be bewildering: 200,000 White Storks (individual flocks can number 11,000 birds), 32,000 Buzzards, 2700 Black Kites, 1600 Lesser Spotted Eagles and 25,000 Honey Buzzards.

In Israel, flocks of hundreds of Buzzards and Tawny Eagles from the Baltic Republics mix with White Storks and Spotted Eagles. These soaring migrants were such a hazard to military aircraft that the Israeli Government commissioned a special study of migration patterns. As a result, military planes now avoid areas where flocks of migrating birds gather.

Farther east, recent expeditions have found an even larger migration route around the eastern end of the Black Sea. Here, 134,000 Buzzards were seen on one day!

Ducks, geese and swans (wildfowl) usually wait for a following wind and cloudless sky before setting off. They fly by both day and night and some, like White-fronted Geese from Greenland, may fly two days non-stop before reaching the British Isles, a journey of over 3400 km. Most migrating wildfowl fly at at about 650 m high, but swans, thought to be migrating Whooper Swans, were seen at a height of over 8000 m by an aircraft pilot!

It is well-known that many land birds cross water when migrating; it is less obvious that many seabirds and waders cross land. Arctic Terns will follow river valleys to take short-cuts to the coast, and waders from west-coast estuaries in northern Britain will frequently cross to the east.

The Grey Phalarope is a wader which breeds in the Arctic and winters on open seas. There is evidence that it travels in the relatively calm waters at the centre of 'depressions' which sweep it along. If a series of depressions from the Atlantic cross Britain in autumn, it is not unusual for Grey

Grey Phalaropes are known in North America as 'gale-birds' because they arrive after bad weather.

Flying in formation saves fuel for geese and other large birds. The bird in front sets up turbulence which helps those that follow.

Phalaropes to be seen around the coasts or scattered across the country.

Small birds usually roost at dusk and are reluctant to fly after dark, but during migration time most activity takes place after dark. For birds making long sea or desert crossings, it is necessary to travel for at least some of the time in the dark, but we do not know why others prefer to do this. It may be because there are fewer predators around, better navigational clues, like stars, and better flying conditions.

Some birds travel in family groups, others migrate in flocks, but some, like Cuckoos, travel alone. Adult Cuckoos leave Europe in July or early August while their young are still in some other bird's nest being cared for by foster parents. The young must also migrate, but they make their journey alone, a few weeks later.

It was also discovered that quite often migrants would use one route in autumn and a different one for their return journey in spring. Lesser Whitethroats and Slender-billed Shearwaters (shown on page 10) do this. White-fronted Geese fly into Britain from the north-east and return to their Arctic breeding grounds by flying almost due east through Europe before turning north from the Moscow region.

Migrating birds usually take the shortest route. Because of the curve of the earth's surface the shortest distance would not be a straight line drawn 'as the crow flies'. Indeed, most migrating birds will follow a curved line, just like aircraft. These imaginary lines are known as Great Circles and Great Circle routes explain why migrants like the Blackpoll Warbler (page 10) fly out over the sea when migrating from North to South America.

Cuckoos (above) migrate to Africa but where exactly our birds go in that great continent is unknown.

Birds, like aircraft, follow Great Circle routes (below).

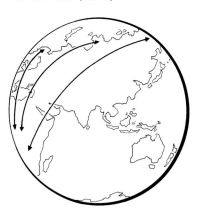

FINDING THEIR WAY

We have seen that birds will travel amazing distances when migrating, but how do they find their way? Swallows fly from one continent to another and still manage to return to the same barn that they nested in the previous year. Whitethroats migrate at night and may fly across the sea in the dark, but still they return to the same breeding sites year after year. How do these birds find their way on their incredible journeys?

The best way of learning the way to a place if you have never been before is to go with someone who knows the route. This is what swans and geese do. The young make their first migration with their parents as a family group, they get to know the route and the best stopping points. It does seem, however, that young swans and geese would be able to migrate alone if they had to.

Birds in flight do have the advantage over animals on the ground in that they have a good view of landmarks such as lakes, hills

Storm Petrels spend the daylight hours at sea and only come to their nest sites at night. The scent from a large colony of Storm Petrels may help them find their way back and identify their individual burrows.

This family of Whooper Swans travelled from their Arctic breeding grounds to winter in western Europe. Adults and young birds travel and winter together.

and coastlines. We know that birds can recognize an area, so a returning young Swallow will remember the village, the barn and even the perch it used the previous year.

Scientists have shown through experiments that the position of the sun in the sky helps migrants to choose the direction in which to fly. They also seem to be able to make allowances for the changing position of the sun during the day.

Migrants do fly at night as well as during the day. They use the clues in the night sky: the different phases of the moon are probably too complicated to be of help, but the patterns of the stars are used to navigate by. This surprising fact was discovered through experimenting with captive birds in a planetarium.

Navigating by the sun during the day and the stars at night cannot be the only clues birds use to find their way. To use the sun and stars birds must have an accurate sense of time. The rotation of the earth every 24 hours means that unless birds can estimate

A Golden Eagle, flying at 2000 m has an excellent view of natural and man-made features. In good weather it will choose a safe place to land and feed.

time to the nearest five minutes they will still not navigate accurately, even if the sky is clear and they recognize the clues.

Some birds get 'lost' in bad weather, but migration does not stop when the sun and the stars are hidden by cloud; and while birds can fly above layers of low cloud, radar studies have shown them continuing to migrate when there is high cloud obscuring the sun and stars. From this, scientists thought that there must be another aid to navigation used by birds and, indeed, by other animals as well.

Recent experiments have shown that some birds obtain information about direction from the Earth's magnetic field. Quite how this works is not fully understood, but a tiny magnetic crystal has been discovered inside pigeon skulls and it may be present in other birds. A 'sixth sense' which allows birds to

Garden Warblers migrate south-west in Europe, but once they cross the Mediterranean they take a different course and fly south.

recognize direction would help to explain many of the mysteries of migration.

There are other senses which birds may use to a greater or lesser extent. Many of the 'tubenosed' seabirds, such as shearwaters, have an extremely good sense of smell and may be able to smell their way home from far out to sea. Land itself can be located this way and the burrows of many of these nocturnal seabirds are very smelly.

Sound may also help migrating birds to find their way. Infra-sound is the name given by scientists to the noises given off by the land. A flying bird may be able to detect the differences in sound between sea and land, mountains and forests, open ocean and rocky coast. These sounds may be audible at a great distance, especially at night. Also, many migrating birds call as they fly. It is generally thought that this keeps flocks together in the dark, but perhaps even their calls sound different when birds are flying over different habitats.

So, there is no simple answer to 'How do birds navigate?' Different species of birds use different methods and most probably use a combination of several. It seems that many birds do not have to learn the direction in which they should migrate or how long they must fly for. This knowledge has evolved and has probably been with a bird since it hatched out of its egg.

FACTS

- An exceptional 'fall' of migrants in Norfolk in 1965 produced, in a 4 km area: 15,000 Redstarts, 8000 Wheatears, 4000 Pied Flycatchers, 3000 Garden Warblers, 1500 Whinchats, 1500 Tree Pipits, 1000 Willow Warblers and 500 Whitethroats!
- Small migrants often fly at a height of 1000 m or more, out of the sight of humans.
- Swans, which have been seen migrating at over 8000 m would experience temperatures of around −48°C.

During experiments with Indigo Buntings in a planetarium in the USA, birds were shown different star maps. Scientists watched how the birds' behaviour altered when they were shown different maps.

Great Shearwaters (left) may be able to smell their way home from far out at sea.

But, while migration may be mostly 'instinctive', birds do learn to change their direction if they are blown off course. In one famous experiment a scientist caught adult and young Starlings in Holland and took them to Switzerland. Normally the Starlings would have left Holland and flown west to England or south-west to northern France for the winter. When released in Switzerland the young birds continued to fly south-west and arrived in the south of France or Spain. The adults, however, corrected their course and generally flew west and north-west, back towards their normal wintering area.

Many birds have to change their direction while migrating so that they can avoid major natural features such as a wide sea crossing or large mountain range. Garden Warblers fly south-west through Europe but, once they have crossed the Mediterranean, they head off due south to their wintering grounds in southern Africa.

Experiments using Garden Warblers in captivity have shown that it is not just the geography of the land that influences the direction these birds fly in. They can also change their direction according to the time of the year. Even when they were kept in captivity in Europe, Garden Warblers changed the direction they wished to fly at about the same time that wild birds would have been flying south through Africa.

MIGRANTS OFF COURSE

Every year, hundreds of millions of Migrants fly from one place to another. Most arrive safely, but a few may be blown off course. Some may migrate in the wrong direction, while others overshoot their target. Many of the migrants which lose their way turn up in unexpected places where they cause lots of excitement among birdwatchers!

Rare vagrants are popular with many birdwatchers. Some, called 'twitchers' will travel hundreds of miles to see a rare bird.

Birds usually wait for the right weather before setting off on migration. If they judge it correctly most small birds will choose light following winds that they can fly in without drifting off course; but they cannot know what weather they will meet on the way. The wrong conditions can ground them, blow them off course or kill them.

Just a small drift off the normal route may take a migrant to quite the wrong place. But lost birds can get back on course. Small migrants, such as Redwings, which may be blown out to sea, will change course, make for land and return to their traditional migration routes. Even larger birds, such as geese, may be blown off course if they run into really rough weather.

A migrant off its course is in danger. It will only have enough fuel (fat) to fly for a certain distance. If its fat is used up before it reaches somewhere safe to stop and feed, it is doomed. Sometimes migrants flying across the sea will land on ships. These tired migrants are a tiny proportion of those which set out, but even this short rest may help them to complete the journey safely. But birds cannot rely on ships; they must make their sea crossings quickly and in the best weather available.

On 11 October 1982, high pressure over Scandinavia and low pressure over Scotland caused the largest fall of migrants seen in this country in recent years. Over 15,000 Goldcrests arrived on the tiny Isle of May in the Firth of Forth, near Edinburgh.

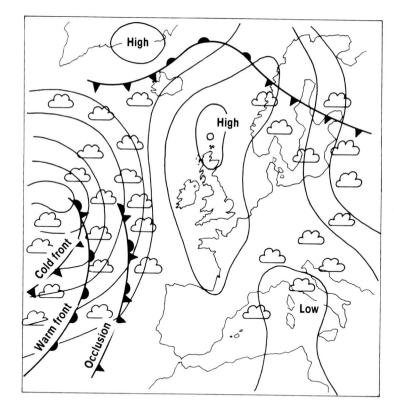

Hoopoes, like this one above, are summer visitors to southern Europe, but a small number reach Britain each spring. Some occasionally stay to nest.

An anticyclone like this will bring problems for migrants crossing the North Sea.

If, in autumn, the television weather forecaster talks about an anticyclone forming over Scandinavia, then cloud will thicken and there will be rain. Migrating birds over the North Sea will run into strong side or head winds and poor visibility. Smaller migrants, especially inexperienced young birds, will become disorientated. Some will land on ships or oil platforms, other will be attracted to the bright lights of lighthouses, but the lucky ones will reorientate themselves and get back on course.

Very occasionally the weather causes amazing arrivals of tired migrants. If there is perfect migration weather when lots of migrants are ready to leave, and on route they encounter rough weather which forces them to land, suddenly thousands of birds may be forced to land on the nearest coast. Birdwatchers call this 'a fall'.

Young migrants on their first journey may be blown off course frequently, but sometimes a few set off in completely the wrong direction! The tiny Pallas's Warbler breeds in central and eastern Asia and winters in south-east Asia, yet their young often turn up on the British east coast in autumn. It seems they set out in the opposite direction. We do not know if they can find their way back again.

Some apparent mistakes can help a species to establish new breeding populations. In spring, it is not unusual for summer migrants to fly farther than their normal breeding areas and arrive farther north. If they then find a suitable nest site they may stay and breed. A good example is the Hoopoe which is a summer migrant to southern Europe. A hundred or so Hoopoes reach Britain each spring, and if a male and female find each other, and a suitable place to nest, they may stay to breed.

Similarly, some winter visitors may not complete their northwards migration and will sometimes try to breed farther south than their normal range. Goldeneyes have recently started breeding in Scotland and have been helped by people putting special nestboxes in forestry plantations. Previously all Goldeneyes returned to northern Scandinavia to breed.

DANGEROUS JOURNEY

It is dangerous being a bird, whatever species, but those that migrate seem to face many more dangers than those that stay in one place for the whole of their lives. Less than half of the migrants that set off in autumn will survive the two journeys and return the following spring. Some of the threats to migrants are natural and have always been there, but others are man-made and very recent. Here, we look at some of the dangers birds face on migration.

Garganeys (above) need small marshy pools for nesting and to feed in before migrating.

When **Swallows** cross the Sahara Desert, they are sometimes forced to shelter from the heat of the mid-day sun. Even the smallest object may used for shade.

A migrant generally sets off when the sky is clear and there is a light, following wind. These are the best conditions for migration for most small birds, and, if it is lucky, the weather will stay good and help the bird on its journey. But, if it encounters bad visibility (fog and cloud) or strong winds, it may become disorientated or be blown off course. If conditions improve, and it still has enough fat reserves, it may be able to find its way back to complete the journey.

As we have seen, it is not unusual for migrants, especially young birds, to be blown off course by bad weather. Being forced off route uses up reserves of fat and the birds become exhausted. If they are over the sea or over a desert when this happens then they are in trouble. If, however, a bird is flying high and visibility improves, its descent may take it to the safety of an island or the shelter of an oasis – but if it doesn't find food and shelter the bird will probably die.

The bright flashes from lighthouses have led many disorientated migrants to their death. On nights when birds are migrating and the weather turns bad, these strong lights attract and dazzle birds which then beat themselves to death against the glass. This problem used to be worse before many

Eleonora's Falcons (above) nest late in the year so that they can feed their young on the small migrants flying south in late summer.

of the towers were floodlit. Now, surrounding bushes are floodlit, too, and tired migrants can rest there until morning.

Scientists once thought that oil rigs in the sea would have the same fatal attraction. But these platforms are probably more helpful because they can provide a temporary resting place for a tired migrant.

More Swallows are found exhausted or dead in the Sahara Desert than any other species because they fly lower than most migrants and get caught in sand storms. Also, if they are blown off course, they have less fat reserves. This is why large numbers of exhausted Swallows are sometimes found sheltering from the sun in an oasis or around oil wells.

If migrants encounter severe storms there will be casualties: hail can kill birds and so can lightning. Storms can be especially severe over the sea and there are records of ships, near a storm, suddenly being covered in exhausted birds. In some parts of the world storms regularly reach hurricane level and the damage to migrants must be enormous.

All birds face threats from natural predators, such as birds of prey, but small migrants crossing the Mediterranean Sea face an additional danger. Eleonora's Falcons, which nest on the cliffs around the Mediterranean, eat small birds. They nest late in the year so that their young will be in the nest, and needing most food, at the time that thousands of young, inexperienced migrants are arriving from northern Europe. The falcons hover and catch tired migrants over land and sea. It is possible that one in every 600 small migrants is caught by an Eleonora's Falcon.

Fog and poor visibility cause difficulties for many migrants but rails and crakes seem to to have special problems. Some

The bright light from a lighthouse can distract disorientated migrants in bad weather. Most lighthouses now have perches for the birds so they do not damage themselves on the windows.

FACTS
■ **Young Swifts may leave their nests, migrate to Africa and return the next spring without ever having landed. They can feed, drink and sleep in flight.**
■ **Brent Geese, which winter in Britain and western Europe, may have come from the north-east or the north-west. Pale-breasted Brent Geese come here from Arctic Canada and dark-breasted come from Siberia.**

fly into buildings and Corncrakes often fly into overhead powerlines. Corncrakes are becoming very rare in western Europe. This hazard could be contributing to their decline.

Small migrants, like Redstarts and migratory ducks such as Garganeys, fly to southern Europe to feed before making a single flight across the Mediterranean and the Sahara. Before setting out they need safe feeding and resting places. Increasingly, the habitats that migrants depend on are being altered by people. Wetlands are drained and the different ways in which land is farmed changes the countryside.

Estuaries are a very important habitat. They are essential for the waders that feed there in winter and also for thousands of other birds that stop to feed before continuing their migration. In western Europe, many estuaries are being developed and changed (for industry, houses, marinas, etc.). Many will soon no longer be safe places for Knots, Sanderlings and other waders as they fly to and from the Arctic.

Even the places where birds fly to can change. In Africa, European migrants, such as Sand Martins and Whitethroats, have been affected by drought. The drought is partly caused by climate change and partly because there are too many people and too much grazing. In the worst years of the

Many estuaries, which provide rich feeding grounds for migrant waders, are under threat. They may have barrages built across them, new ports built on them or other developments, like marinas, which will destroy valuable bird habitats.

drought, the number of Whitethroats returning to Britain fell by 75 per cent.

Hunting migrants is still common in many Mediterranean countries like Italy, Greece and Malta. It is estimated that over one hundred million migrant birds are shot or trapped each year.

Laws to protect these migrants, especially the rarer species, have been passed in most countries. But these laws are almost impossible to enforce and are completely ignored by the hunters.

Small birds like Robins and Blackcaps are trapped and eaten as a delicacy, but birds of prey, such as Honey Buzzards, and other larger species, are shot for no reason except that the hunters love killing. Unlike legal hunting in Britain and other countries, the people who hunt migrants in southern Europe do not limit their hunting to those species that have healthy populations. They shoot and trap anything.

There used to be a healthy population of Roseate Terns in Western Europe but they have declined rapidly. On the west coast of

Africa they are caught, along with some other seabirds, by young children with fishing line. Again, they are not caught for food, it is just a game. In Ghana, Wildlife Clubs are being formed in schools to educate young people to appreciate their country's birds and the other wildlife.

Seabirds face another potential hazard – pollution. Oil gets into the sea from many sources, especially from tankers accidentally or deliberately discharging oil from their tanks. Migration routes cross popular shipping lanes and it is quite common for seabirds to get oil on their feathers. Once oiled there is little hope for the birds and they die.

Being free to migrate across continents is not always an advantage – almost half the migrating birds will die. But the survivors are fitter and ready to breed in an area where food is plentiful. They pass on the will to migrate to the next generation.

Millions of small birds like this Blackcap (below), are trapped and killed every year as they migrate through the Mediterranean region.

Oil at sea is a hidden danger for birds (below). Once they are oiled, they most probably will die.

In West Africa, small boys catch and kill terns for fun (above), but the Wildlife Clubs of Ghana are showing children that these birds need conserving.

STUDYING MIGRATION

Many of the mysteries of bird migration have been solved during the twentieth century – or have they? Like so much of science, the more that is discovered the more questions are raised. There are still gaps in our knowledge which ornithologists are trying to fill. The more we understand about birds and the way they behave, the more we can help to conserve them.

Methods of studying birds have gradually been developed during the twentieth century. The most usual method is to fit a light-weight metal ring to a leg of the bird being studied. This ring has a unique set of numbers and letters embossed on it so that wherever that bird goes, it carries its personal identity with it. If a bird is retrapped, or found dead, the original ringing information can be compared with the new data to find out how long it survived and how far it travelled.

Unfortunately, very few birds are seen after they have had a ring fitted, especially the small migrants which fly to Africa. But a small proportion of rings are recovered and

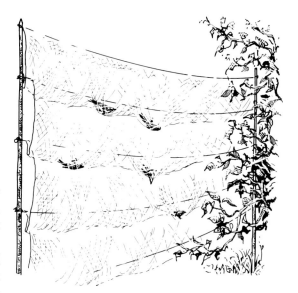

Some ornithologists put up mist nets to catch migrating birds which they then weigh, measure and ring. The birds are not harmed by this process and the records are important.

A Heligoland trap (below) is often used by bird observatories to catch small migrants. Again, the birds are not harmed.

Different rings and special pliers are used to tag birds ranging from Goldcrests to Mute Swans.

People who ring birds are specially trained so the bird is not injured and can live a normal life, wearing its ring, after release.

international records are passed on to the country of origin. We are gradually learning about the breeding or wintering areas of most of the common species.

There are still some surprising mysteries. House Martins are common birds in Europe during the spring and summer. Ninety million are thought to enter Africa each autumn, but exactly where they go is still largely unknown.

The whereabouts of British House Martins is a particular mystery: it was always suspected that they crossed the Sahara and wintered in central Africa, but it was not until 1986, after 150,000 House Martins had been ringed, that one British-ringed bird was found in northern Nigeria. It is suspected that most House Martins spend their winter flying at high altitudes in central Africa and seldom come down to near ground level, even to sleep.

Catching birds to ring them requires great care and must only be carried out by people who have been specially trained. In Britain and many other countries, bird ringers not only have to have lengthy training, they also need to apply for a special government department license.

The usual way to catch small birds is in a mist net. The net is so fine that the birds do not see it. They fly into it and are held secure before being removed by a ringer. Once out of the net, the birds are identified, measured, weighed, and they have their plumage checked so that age, sex and moult can be recorded. Once these details have been noted on special forms the ring is fitted to a leg using special pliers, the ring number is recorded and the bird released.

Some birds are caught in special traps. The Heligoland trap is often used near the coast for catching migrants. Named after the island where it was first used, it allows birds to feed and shelter right up to the moment they are captured.

Another way to catch birds is to use a cannon net (or rocket net). Cannon nets are used to catch flocks of larger birds such as geese and waders. Rolled and camouflaged nets are set around a place where birds regularly feed or roost then, when the birds are in position, rockets are fired which carry the net over the whole flock.

At various points around the coast there are bird observatories. Ringing takes place here regularly during migration, birds are

Cannon netting is an exciting and harmless way to catch large birds, such as geese.

The yellow necks on these Whooper Swans are caused by a coloured dye. This allows them to be recognized and studied.

counted and bird migration is studied. Some observatories have full-time staff, and they encourage other birdwatchers to go and stay to help them with their work.

Of course, many birds are ringed in their nests. This has to be done especially carefully, but it does have the advantage of helping the ringer to work out the exact age of the birds.

Sometimes ringers make special journeys to ring particular birds or to record migration at a special location. Expeditions to the Arctic to ring Pink-footed Geese or Ringed Plovers can tell us much about the habitats these birds use and their migrations. Other ringing schemes have been set up by British ornithologists: the Mediterranean island of Mallorca and Senegal in west Africa have both been used as sites for special studies of migrants.

With so much work going into ringing birds it is a pity that so few are recovered, but we can all help. It is usually impossible to read the ring number on the leg of a live bird but when a bird is dead the ring can be removed and the details sent to the address on the ring, which is usually a museum. The organizers will need to know where and when the ring was found, how the bird died (if known), the species of bird and your own name and address. If you send this information you will probably receive a computer print-out giving all

Radio tracking allows field workers to follow all the movements of a bird, however secretive. Here, an ornithologist is tracking a Corncrake.

the details of the bird, including when and where it was originally ringed.

Ringing is not the only scientific method used to study migration. For some studies, coloured dyes are used to mark feathers. The birds with patches of bright colour, are easy to see at a distance and their migration routes can be mapped. Colour marking is much easier to see than a metal ring, but the dye will only last until the bird's next moult.

Another technique is to 'tag' birds with a tiny radio transmitter which sends out a signal that can be picked up by a receiver. This

Many volunteers like to spend their holiday counting the thousands of birds of prey which migrate through Israel each autumn.

allows scientists to follow the daily journeys of the marked bird. Usually, these transmitters are used on resident species, but migratory movements can be detected.

In the northern valleys of Israel, birdwatchers from many countries help local ornithologists to count birds of prey, storks and pelicans during their autumn migration. Spaced out across an area, birdwatchers count vast numbers of birds which rise on the thermals throughout the daylight hours every day between mid August and mid-October (see page 23). Studies like this not only tell us what route migrants are taking. they show how their populations change from year to year.

Another way to watch migrating birds is from aircraft. This can be difficult, though, because planes travel faster than birds. Some pilots have seen high-flying migrants such as swifts and swans, and ornithologists using light aircraft have followed radio-tagged birds. Gliders have even joined flocks of storks and birds of prey to ride the thermals with them!

YOUR OWN MIGRATION PROJECTS

Ornithology is a science where amateurs and professionals work together. Much of our knowledge has come from birdwatchers who record what they see or from people who give up their spare time to ring or count birds. As migrants fly to nearly every part of the Earth's surface there is no reason why you should not start your own studies – wherever you live.

It used to be fashionable, in Britain, to write to *The Times* newspaper when the first Cuckoo of the year was heard. They seldom make the news these days, but people are still excited by seeing a early migrant. It's a sign that summer is on the way.

Counting your local birds regularly can reveal local migrations and seasonal changes in numbers. A good place to do this is at your nearest reservoir or lake.

First Dates

Most birdwatchers keep a field notebook. There are lots of different ways to keep notes but you should always record first sightings of early migrants quickly before you forget the important information.

The date, place (including grid reference – you can get this from an Ordnance Survey map), time and weather are all important, especially if you are going to send the information to your local natural history society or bird club.

A migrant arrival chart

A migrant chart is a simple way to record the arrival dates of the migrating birds that visit your local area. Go out regularly from late winter and during the spring. Remember to look out for migrants on your regular journeys to and from school, or on visits to local parks. Try to birdwatch early

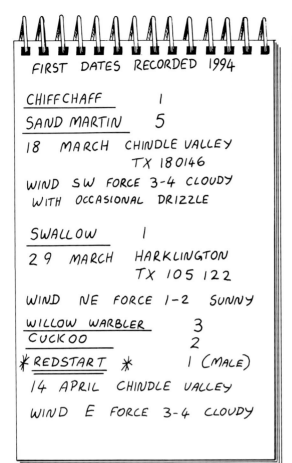

This birdwatcher's notebook shows entries for summer migrants and the things you should note.

DATE	MARCH 18	19	25	26	31	1	6	APRIL 7	13	14	19	20	21	28	30	MAY 2	3	8
LITTLE RINGED PLOVER	1				1	1	2	3	2									
SAND MARTIN		8				3		5	11		8	20	42					
HOUSE MARTIN			2								6	20						
SWALLOW										1	4	27	20	10				
YELLOW WAGTAIL			2	1			4				2	10	4					
CHIFFCHAFF	1	1	2	1	1	4	1	1										
WILLOW WARBLER								1			1	4						
BLACKCAP								2			2	6	4					
CUCKOO													1	1	2			
SWIFT															28			

SUMMER MIGRANTS RUNDLE MOSS 1994

A migration arrival chart.

Then you can compare the arrival dates and see which weather conditions are likely to bring migrants to your area.

Latest dates

A lot of attention is given to the arrival dates of spring migrants. The leaving dates and the weather at the time are also fascinating but generally under-recorded. The methods of recording last dates are similar those for recording first dates.

A study area

Many of us do not live in an area where there are large numbers of migrants, but you will probably have a local site where birds gather or where a few migrants stop on their way through. This site could be a local park, a piece of farmland, a gravel pit, a nature reserve or a country park. Each of these places can make great study areas.

Arrange to visit your study area at regular intervals. Morning visits are particularly valuable. Choose a route that you can take every time. And, do not forget to take a notebook with you to record everything that you see, even the numbers of common birds.

in the morning when birds are most active and visit any places that could be attractive to migrants.

Make up a chart, like the one above, and make a list of the migrants you see. Write on the number of migrants you see each day during the main migration period. Once a particular species has arrived, stop recording it and concentrate on the others. Keep a simple summary of the weather at the time, especially wind direction.

A completed chart is a valuable record and you should send a copy of the information to the person who collects bird reports for your area. You'll find the name and address of your local bird recorder at your local library.

Migrant charts become even more valuable if you keep them from year to year.

Soon, you will become an expert on your local patch and will see how the numbers of birds change from week to week. Some of these changes will be because of the arrival and departure of summer and winter migrants like Blackcaps or Fieldfares. But other changes will be a result of partial migration: there may be more Coots in your local park after others have arrived from the continent; Meadow Pipits may pass through in autumn and spring as they move from uplands to lowlands and back.

Local studies are the basis of ornithology and can have unexpected uses. Accurate records taken over a period of time are invaluable if the site is ever threatened by

Key • **First record** ▓ **Main arrival**

Years	10	11	12	13	14	15	16	17	18
91				•		▓	▓	▓	▓
90		•				▓	▓	▓	▓
89			•			▓	▓	▓	▓
88			•		▓	▓	▓	▓	▓
87				•		▓	▓	▓	▓
86					•	▓	▓	▓	▓
85					•	▓	▓	▓	▓
84					•	▓	▓	▓	▓

Weeks 10 11 12 13 14 15 16 17 18

← **March** → ← **April** →

The graph on the left shows that, while migrating Willow Warblers arrive in spring, the dates can vary from year to year.

Sea-watching

development. Your records could help to save a place that migrating birds depend on to rest during their long distance flights.

Desk work

Most local bird clubs and natural history societies publish regular reports of summer, winter and passage migrants in their area. These should be available in your local library.

Choose a few species and draw bar charts to show when they arrive and depart. Bar charts will show when passage migrants move through your area. One helpful hint is to divide each year into the 52 weeks and use these for your bar charts (see diagram).

Listening for migrants

Redwing migration often takes place on clear nights in October and November. If you are outside on a clear autumn evening, listen for the high-pitched 'seee' call of Redwings.

Sea-watching

The migration routes of many seabirds brings them close to the shores of western Europe. Bad weather or strong winds will often mean you will see more seabirds.

To master the art of sea-watching, you need to practise and have patience. Ideally, there should be two of you and it is helpful, but not necessary, to have a telescope.

Find a comfortable position for sitting and looking out to sea – the top of a shingle bank or a safe cliff-top – and be prepared to wait for a while. Scan the sea for swimming birds and note any you see. Watch carefully because it is easy to miss birds hidden between waves. Keep your binoculars trained on and below the horizon to look for flying birds or new ones which may swim into view.

You may find it easier to ignore the common species of gulls.

If you are lucky and there are lots of seabirds, one person should identify the birds and call them out to the other who takes notes. The direction in which birds are moving is important so try to give directions like this: 'one Gannet north, two Kittiwakes north, one diver south, etc'. You could use arrows as a shorthand instead of writing directions.

To get the best out of your sea-watching, take it in turns to watch and take notes.

This graph (below) shows the pattern of Ospreys (far left) migrating through Bedfordshire.

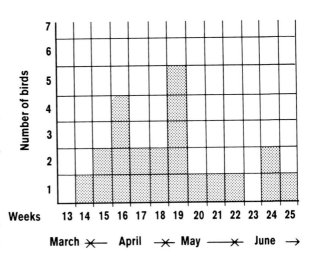

OTHER MIGRANTS

If someone mentions migration, people generally think of birds. That is not surprising because bird migration has fascinated many people for centuries. There can be very few people who are unaware of at least some birds that migrate. Birds are not the only creatures that migrate, though. Many others make these seasonal movements. They may not cover the same great distances, but they are still spectacular in their own way. Here, we take a look at a few.

Insect migration

Many insects travel surprisingly long distances to find new sources of food and to colonize new places. Most insects travel through the air and rely on air currents and wind direction. However, such travel, marvellous though it is, is not true migration. The insects do not return to where they started and their journeys tend to be accidental rather than deliberate.

Some insects really do migrate, though: Red Admirals, Painted Ladies and Clouded Yellows are all butterflies that migrate northwards through Europe in spring. They cannot usually survive a British winter, but each spring they make their way north and reach the British Isles in varying numbers. Some will stay here to breed and there are a few reports of these butterflies flying south again in the autumn.

Another well-known butterfly migrant is the Monarch butterfly (see the picture **above**). This butterfly is common over most of North America and every autumn tens of thousands fly south to spend the winter in sub-tropical conditions.

Once they are there, they hang together in masses on trees in a state of semi-hibernation. In spring, they make their way north again. They lay their eggs in the middle altitudes and the young that hatch then carry on the journey north. In the autumn, they return south.

Eels and Salmon

Eels (**above right**) are fish. They breed in the sea and the young of some species migrate to freshwater rivers where they grow into adults. Those that live in European rivers, return to the Sargasso Sea near the West Indies to breed and their young then travel to the same traditional rivers in Europe.

Salmon (**above left**) behave quite differently. They breed in rivers but spend part of their lives at sea. They only come back when they are ready to breed.

Wildebeest

Great herds of Wildebeests (**above**) live on the grasslands of Africa but their food supply depends on the rains. Wildebeests undergo long migrations to reach reach suitable feeding areas and their journeys take them along traditional routes which cross fast-flowing rivers and through countryside where there is no food.

Toads and Turtles

Toads (**left**) need water to breed. For much of the year they live away from water and, at the first sign of spring, they migrate to their breeding ponds – often in huge numbers.

Some turtles (**above**) live out at sea, but need to come ashore to lay their eggs. They have favourite, traditional beaches where they bury their eggs. They migrate to these beaches year after year.

Great whales

These huge mammals are found in all the oceans. As they are studied by scientists we are discovering that they, too, have set migration routes.

Humpback Whales (**below**) give birth in warm sub-tropical seas. There is one population around Hawaii and another near the West Indies. In late summer, after breeding, these whales migrate northwards to rich feeding grounds on the edge of the Arctic. The Hawaiian whales swim to the waters off the coast of Alaska and the West Indian whales move north to feed on the Grand Banks off the east coast of America before continuing farther north to fishing grounds off Labrador.

GLOSSARY

Altitudinal Migration – migration up or down hill, which often has the same benefits for the species as long distance migration.

Brood – Young birds of one family, all from one clutch of eggs.

Eruption – Irregular one-way movement away from an area of high population, often triggered by food shortage.

Habitat – An area which has a distinct form of vegetation and is home to a distinct variety of birds and other animals.

Hibernate – Becoming dormant (sleeping) for a period of time.

Invasion – An unusually large movement of birds into an area, usually for a short period of time, often triggered by lack of food.

Irruption – The arrival of birds from an area where the population is higher, usually caused by shortage of food.

Juvenile – A young bird out of the nest but retaining some of its first plumage.

Leap-frog Migration – Where some birds, after breeding, migrate through the area occupied by others of the same species and then fly on further to their winter quarters.

Migration – The movement from one area to another, followed, at another season by a return journey.

Moult – The natural loss and replacement of feathers. Usually an annual event.

Moult Migration – The movement to a special area for the purpose and duration of moult.

Partial Migrant – A species where some of the population migrate and others do not.

Passage Migrant – A bird which passes through an area on its migratory journey.

Predator – A bird or animal which feeds on other species.

Raptor – Day-flying bird of prey.

Resident – A bird which remains in the same area through out the year.

Soaring – Circling flight, apparently without effort, often in thermals of warm air.

Summer Migrant – a bird which arrives in its breeding area in spring and leaves in late summer or autumn.

Species – An animal or plant of one type which is capable of reproducing a new generation identical to its self.

Territories – A place where a bird or other animal lives and which it may defend from others of the same species.

Thermal – Rising column of warm air, often used by birds to gain height with the minimum effort.

Wildfowl – Ducks, geese and swans.

Winter Migrant – A bird which arrives in autumn and leaves in late winter or early spring and breeds elsewhere.

NDEX

A

Arctic Fox 12, 13
Arctic Tern 6, 8, 9, 11, 22, 24
Arctic Warbler 21

B

Barnacle Goose 12, 13
Barn Swallow 21
Bar-tailed Godwit 19
Bewick's Swan 11, 12
Blackcap 17, 34, 42
Black Kite 23, 24
Blackpoll Warbler 10, 25
Brambling 20
Brent Goose 33
Buzzard 23, 24

C

Chiffchaff 16
Clouded Yellow 44
Coot 42
Cormorant 23
Corncrake 5, 16, 34, 38
Crane 14, 23
Crested Tit 20
Crossbill 9,14
Cuckoo 14, 16, 17, 25, 40

D

Dotterel 12

E

Eagle 23
Eel 44
Eleonora's Falcon 33

F

Fieldfare 19, 42

G

Gannet 13, 43
Garden Warbler 28, 29
Garganey 16, 32, 34
Goldcrest 30, 37
Golden Eagle 27
Goldeneye 18, 31
Great Shearwater 8
Great Spotted Woodpecker 19
Grey Phalarope 24, 25
Grey Plover 19
Grey Wagtail 8

H

Honey Buzzard 23, 24, 34
Hoopoe 31
House Martin 17, 37
Humpback Whale 45

I

Indigo Bunting 29

K

Kite 14
Kittiwake 9, 43
Knot 19, 34

L

Lapwing 9, 18
Lesser Spotted Eagle 24
Lesser Whitethroat 25
Long-tailed Duck 12

M

Manx Shearwater 8, 9, 29
Meadow Pipit 42
Monarch Butterfly 44
Mute Swan 37

N

Nile 14, 15
Nightingale 5, 16

O

Osprey 13, 42

P

Painted Lady 44
Pallas's Warbler 31
Pelican 23, 39
Pied Flycatcher 23, 24
Pigeon 27
Pink-footed Goose 38
Pochard 5, 7

R

Red Admiral 44
Redstart 14, 34
Redwing 6, 19, 25, 30, 43
Red-breasted Goose 14
Reed Warbler 17
Ringed Plover 8, 38
Robin 6, 14, 34
Roseate Tern 34
Ruby-throated Hummingbird 10, 23

S

Salmon 44
Sanderling 34
Sand Martin 17, 34
Sedge Warbler 16, 22, 23
Shearwater 28
Shelduck 8, 9
Short-eared Owl 18
Shoveler 18
Slender-billed Shearwater 10, 25
Snow Bunting 12, 13
Spotted Eagle 24
Spotted Flycatcher 17
Starling 29
Stork 23, 39
Storm Petrel 26
Swallow 5, 6, 14, 15, 16, 17, 20, 21, 22, 26, 32, 33, 38
Swan 39
Swift 16, 17, 20, 33, 39

T

Tawny Eagle 24
Toad 45
Turtle 45
Turtle Dove 14

W

Waxwing 9
Wheatear 6, 11, 16, 20, 21, 38
Whimbrel 19
White-fronted Goose 14, 24, 25
White Stork 14, 24
Whitethroat 26, 34
Whooper Swan 18, 24, 26, 38
Wildebeest 45
Wildfowl 24
Willow Warbler 12, 16, 20, 21

The photographs are copyright and are produced by kind permission of:

p.8 G McCarthy (RSPB); p.9 (lt), 12, 24, 32 P Sterry (Nature Photographers Ltd); 9 (rt), 35 (lt), C H Gomersall (RSPB); p.14 (lt) Reed International Books (British Museum); p.14 (rt) Sir Eric Eastwood (Marconi Company); p.20 E A Janes (RSPB); p.25 K Carlson (Nature Photographers Ltd); p.26, 38, 39 R Tidman (Nature Photographers Ltd); p.29 R Tidman; p.30 A Cleave (Nature Photographers Ltd); p.31 J Hancock (Nature Photographers Ltd); p.35 (rt top) M Gore (Nature Photographers Ltd); p.35 (bottom rt) C H Gomersall (Nature Photographers Ltd); p.37 (lt) D Smith (Nature Photographers Ltd); p.37 (rt) C Mead.